CALF, GOODNIGHT

CALF, GOODNIGHT

by Nancy Jewell

Pictures by Leonard Weisgard

Harper & Row, Publishers
New York, Evanston, San Francisco, London

CALF, GOODNIGHT

Text copyright © 1973 by Nancy Jewell
Illustrations copyright © 1973 by Leonard Weisgard

All rights reserved. No part of this book may be used or reproduced in any manner whatsoever without written permission except in the case of brief quotations embodied in critical articles and reviews. Printed in the United States of America. For information address Harper & Row, Publishers, Inc., 10 East 53rd Street, New York, N.Y. 10022. Published simultaneously in Canada by Fitzhenry & Whiteside Limited, Toronto.

Library of Congress Catalog Card Number: 72–9856
Trade Standard Book Number: 06–022829–6
Harpercrest Standard Book Number: 06–022830–X

FIRST EDITION

For my parents, Ruth and Russell Jewell
and my sister, Barbara Jewell Ritchie

"Night is coming," said Mama Cow,
nudging her small new calf,
"and we must be starting for the barn."
"What is night?" asked Calf,
digging his hooves deeper into the cool wet grass.
"Night," said Mama Cow, "is when the sun goes down,
and cows go back to the barn to sleep."
And she nudged Calf again as they moved slowly
toward the barn at the end of the field.

"I think I like night," said Calf,
feeling suddenly excited.
"And I think I would like to stay outside
and not go to sleep at all."
But he kept following Mama Cow.
Her breath smelled warm and sweet.
She made a *swish-swish* sound
as she walked through the grass.

"Who are you?" Calf asked,
looking up at something milky and round high in the sky.
"That is the moon," said Mama Cow.
"The moon is part of the night too.
And so is going to sleep in a nice warm barn."
"I think I will stay outside with the moon," said Calf.
But the moon looked cold and far away.
"I want to spend the night in the barn after all,"
said Calf, hurrying to catch up with his mother.

"Nonsense," hissed a small furry creature
rushing through the grass.
"Night is for running under the moon with other cats."
The wind rustled the trees.
"I will run with you too!" called Calf.
Mama Cow turned all the way around
and gave Calf a long, long look.
"Never mind!" he shouted.
"I am going to spend the night
in the barn with the cows."

Something went *whoo-oo-oo-oo*
from a big dark tree near Calf.
"That is only a hoot owl,"
said Mama Cow as Calf drew closer to her.
"Owls are part of the night too."
"Night," hooted Owl,
"is owl eyes glowing in the dark
and owl voices calling *whoo-oo-oo-oo-oo*.
Night-time is owl-time."
"O-o-o-h!" said Calf, shivering a little.

Tiny lights gleamed all over the sky.
"Who are you?" called Calf,
stretching his neck so he could see way up high.
"They are the stars," mooed Mama Cow.
"And when the stars come out in the sky
that is time for little calves and big cows
to be asleep in the barn."
And she gave Calf a poke with her warm muzzle.
"I would love to stay outside with the stars!" Calf sighed.
But the stars looked even farther away than the moon,
and Calf walked faster to catch up with Mama Cow.

Then something big galloped by Calf.
"Who are you?" he shouted,
wanting to run after it.
"That," said Mama Cow, "is a dog,
and you are a calf,
and if you don't hurry,
you will soon be a cross and sleepy calf
with a cross and sleepy mother."
For a while Calf walked right at Mama Cow's side.
Then there was a new sound!

Calf stopped.
"What is that?" he asked.
"Only another silly dog," said Mama Cow.
"Now hurry along."
"But what is he doing?" asked Calf.
"He is howling," said Mama Cow.
"Dogs are foolish creatures who howl at night."
"Night," barked the dog,
"is for howling and howling and howling
until someone howls back!"

Calf tried hard to howl back.
"Move along, my little dog-calf," said Mama Cow.
"I'm coming!" yelled Calf.
And he kicked up his heels because
the cold night air felt so good.
He ran right past Mama Cow.

"Watch out,"
grunted something from deep in the grass.
"Where are you?" said Calf.
"And who are you?"
"I am Mole,
and I am digging a hole near your left hoof
so I can burrow into the warm earth."
"That is nice," said Calf.
"But I want to stay on top of the ground."

Then he saw a warm yellow light
very low in the sky.
"There is a star I can touch!" said Calf.
And he ran right up to it.
"Where are you, Mama Cow?" yelled Calf.
"Come see the star!"

"That is a lantern, my little calf," said Mama Cow,
as she caught up with him.
She pushed him gently
through the open door of the building.

"How warm it is," said Calf.
"I wish we could go to sleep right here
and not have to go to the barn."
"We are in the barn," said Mama Cow,
licking Calf on his face.
But Calf didn't hear her.
He was sound asleep in a big pile of hay.

Withdrawn

CHURCH LIBRARY
WATERFORD MENNONITE